Original title:
The Feeling Rainbow

Copyright © 2024 Creative Arts Management OÜ
All rights reserved.

Author: Mariana Leclair
ISBN HARDBACK: 978-9916-88-974-9
ISBN PAPERBACK: 978-9916-88-975-6

Revelations in Rainbow

Colors whisper secrets bright,
In the sky, a fleeting sight.
Each hue unveils a new day,
Painting dreams that softly sway.

Nature's brush strokes high above,
Crafting tales of peace and love.
Under arches, hearts align,
In the spectrum, souls entwine.

Emblem of Emotions

In each gesture, feelings rise,
Hidden truths behind our eyes.
Words unspoken, shadows cast,
Emotions flow, both deep and vast.

Fragile hearts in silent dance,
Finding solace in a glance.
Every heartbeat sings a song,
In this emblem, we belong.

Dreams Painted in Pastels

Softly hues in twilight gleam,
Brushing canvases of dream.
Whispers of a secret place,
Where fantasies find their grace.

Gentle thoughts in muted tones,
In this realm, we're not alone.
Every vision, calm and free,
Shadows fade, and we can see.

Celestial Constellations of Care

Stars align in night's embrace,
Guiding hearts to find their place.
In the dark, a lantern's glow,
Constellations care and know.

Infinite in every spark,
Lengthening paths through the dark.
We are stardust, born of light,
In connection, our true might.

Vibration of Joyful Shadows

In twilight's embrace, shadows dance free,
Whispers of laughter, a soft jubilee.
Each flicker of light, in colors entwined,
Echoes of joy, in the heart of the mind.

Beneath the starlight, dreams start to play,
Moments suspended, in night's gentle sway.
The pulse of the earth in a melody glows,
Vibrations of love, where the spirit flows.

Radiant Waves of Memory

Upon the shoreline, memories crest,
Radiant waves in the sunset's nest.
Carried by tides, a story unfolds,
Whispers of ages, in blue and gold.

Each grain of sand holds a moment so dear,
A dance of the past, forever near.
Like ripples that shimmer under the sun,
Waves of recollection, eternally spun.

A Canvas of Hope and Heartache

Brush strokes of sorrow, mixed with delight,
Create a portrait in shades of the night.
Colors that clash, then harmonize true,
A canvas of heartache and hope shining through.

In every hue lies a story to tell,
Of fortunes once lost and triumphs that dwell.
With every stroke, a new path is drawn,
A tapestry rich, from dusk until dawn.

Ripples of Luminous Yearning

Beneath the surface, a longing resides,
Ripples of dreams in the ocean's tides.
Each wave whispers softly, a call to explore,
A luminous journey, revealing much more.

In depths of the night, where starlight ignites,
Yearning expands, with the moon's gentle sights.
Emerging in waves, a pulse from the deep,
Awakening spirits, in twilight's sweet sleep.

Emotion's Ebb and Flow

In shadows deep, the feelings rise,
Tides of joy, then waves of sighs.
A heart that dances, soft and slow,
Caught in the rhythm, the ebb and flow.

A tender glance, a fleeting touch,
Moments fleeting, yet they mean so much.
With every heartbeat, stories unfold,
In the silence, emotions bold.

The whispers of love, the pang of pain,
Sunlit memories, the drenching rain.
Through tempests raging, we find our way,
Guided by stars, through night and day.

In every heartbeat, a tale to tell,
Of soaring heights and shadowed dwell.
Emotion's journey, wild and free,
A timeless dance, just you and me.

Serenity in Spectrum

Beneath the sky, where colors blend,
A tranquil heart begins to mend.
With every hue, a story we weave,
In shades of peace, we learn to believe.

The golden rays of morning light,
Brush away remnants of the night.
In lavender fields, the whispers play,
Their gentle tones lead us on our way.

Azure waves against the shore,
Echo the dreams we yearn for more.
In crimson sunsets, the world stands still,
Filling our hearts with a quiet thrill.

Through every color, a moment seen,
In the spectrum's arms, we find serene.
A tapestry woven, soft and bright,
Bringing solace in the fading light.

Tints of Fleeting Moments

In the twilight's gentle glow,
Colors fade, whispers flow.
Time dances on a breeze,
Ephemeral as autumn leaves.

Each fleeting shade we trace,
In memories, we find our place.
Moments blink, then they're gone,
The heart holds what lingers on.

Threads of Vibrant Longing

In the silence of the night,
A yearning pulls, soft and light.
Threads woven, dreams ignite,
Colors swirling, pure delight.

With each heartbeat, passion calls,
Through the shadows, hope enthralls.
In the tapestry of the soul,
Longing whispers, makes us whole.

Murmurs of Serene Tones

In the stillness, soft and pure,
Murmurs echo, hearts endure.
Gentle breezes, whispered sighs,
Underneath the starlit skies.

Colors blend in muted grace,
In the silence, find your place.
Serenity in every sound,
In these tones, our peace is found.

Brushstrokes of Timeless Emotions

With each stroke, feelings bloom,
On the canvas, dispel the gloom.
Brushes dance, colors collide,
In this art, hearts confide.

Timeless moments, captured bright,
Fleeting shadows, shimmer light.
Emotions painted, rich and deep,
In this masterpiece, we keep.

Emotional Tapestries

Threads of joy weave through my heart,
In shadows cast by love's sweet art.
Each color tells a secret tale,
Of dreams that soar, or hopes that fail.

The fabric frays, yet still stands strong,
Whispers of right, and echoes of wrong.
Stitched with laughter, sewn with tears,
A tapestry of all my years.

Together we create the scene,
In vibrant hues, both harsh and clean.
Interwoven moments shared side by side,
A journey's map, where hearts abide.

In every stitch, a memory found,
In every layer, love's sound resounds.
Emotional threads forever entwined,
In the tapestry of hearts aligned.

Luminaries of Love

Stars ignite in the velvet night,
Each one a spark, a beacon of light.
Guiding lost souls through darkened skies,
Whispering truths that never die.

Moments of passion, a flickering flame,
In shadows deep, they still proclaim.
Love's light shines in the depths of despair,
A glow that reassures, a warmth we share.

Together, we dance in the glow of the moon,
Each heartbeat synced, a lasting tune.
Luminaries cast in the vastness above,
Each twinkle a promise, a symbol of love.

In the embrace of the cosmos wide,
We find our peace, with hearts open wide.
Guided by light, always in sight,
Luminaries shining, our eternal night.

Cosmic Colorwheel

In the vast expanse where dreams collide,
Colors blend and emotions reside.
Spirals of wonder swirl and dance,
Inviting all for a second chance.

Crimson for passion, blue for the calm,
Swirling together, a soothing balm.
Yellow rays spark joy from within,
A palette of feelings where love begins.

Through cosmic strokes, we paint our fate,
Each hue a memory that we create.
In the colorwheel, our spirits play,
A universe built from night and day.

Together we blend in this vibrant space,
Crafting a masterpiece, a warm embrace.
Every shade holds a tale untold,
In this cosmic canvas, our hearts unfold.

Surges of Sparkle

Tiny glimmers in the morning dew,
Each one a story, a dream to pursue.
Surges of sparkle light up the day,
Chasing the shadows, keeping gloom at bay.

In laughter shared, a flicker ignites,
Illuminating paths, replacing the nights.
Moments of magic in the simplest things,
The joy that each little sparkle brings.

With eyes like lanterns, we find our way,
Through winding roads, bright as the fray.
The universe twinkles with playful delight,
Surges of sparkle dance into the night.

In the rhythm of life, we find the glow,
Connection that ebbs with each ebb and flow.
Surges of sparkle in every embrace,
A reminder that love's light fills the space.

Sinfonia of a Thousand Shades

In the cradle of twilight's embrace,
Colors dance in a gentle trace.
Whispers of dreams take to the sky,
Each note a heartbeat, a soft sigh.

Brushstrokes of silence in the night,
Melodies weave in ethereal light.
A symphony played on whispers made,
In the stillness, my fears allayed.

Every hue tells a story anew,
Bold; yet tender, a soft, vivid hue.
The canvas of dusk, a masterpiece,
Where the heart finds solace, a sweet peace.

With a thousand shades, we move as one,
In the fleeting glow of the setting sun.
Our souls intertwined, a perfect blend,
In this sinfonia, we transcend.

Brightness Beyond the Veil

In shadows deep, a flicker shines,
A truth concealed in silent lines.
Beyond the veil where dreams reside,
A beacon calls from the other side.

With every breath, a whisper glows,
A promise wrapped in sacred prose.
Hope dances lightly on the breeze,
In the heart's chambers, it finds ease.

The light cascades, a gentle stream,
Washing over fears like a dream.
In the depth of night, it starts to swell,
A warmth ignites; it's time to dwell.

So lift your gaze where the stars unfold,
Within the warmth, find stories told.
Beyond the veil, where brightness reigns,
Awakening love in lingering chains.

Harmonies of Light and Shadow

In the balance of bright and dark,
A dance unfolds, igniting a spark.
Echoes of laughter, whispers of pain,
In the harmonies, joy can remain.

Colors entwined in a spectral waltz,
Shadows embrace, revealing their faults.
Every heartbeat sings a refrain,
Together existing, a sweet domain.

Light takes the lead while shadows sigh,
A duet sung beneath the sky.
In the flicker of dusk, they collide,
Creating a story where worlds abide.

So let the melodies guide your way,
In the dance of night and day.
For in this harmony, we will find,
A peace that lingers, a bond entwined.

Whirlwind of Celestial Hues

In a whirlwind filled with colors bright,
Celestial whispers take their flight.
Galaxies twirl in an endless spin,
Inviting dreams where we begin.

Soft winds carry stardust fair,
With every swirl, a silent prayer.
The cosmos hums a vibrant tune,
Under the watchful gaze of the moon.

Infinite echoes paint the sky,
As comets race and meteors fly.
In this dance of space and time,
Our spirits soar, our hearts in rhyme.

So let us twirl in this cosmic gale,
Among the stars, we will set sail.
In a whirlwind of hues, we align,
Bound by the beauty of the divine.

Echoes of Euphoria

In the laughter of the trees,
Joy dances on whispers soft.
With each heartbeat, it flows,
A melody of dreams aloft.

Moments freeze in golden sun,
Each second a treasure rare.
We chase the light, feeling free,
In the warmth of the summer air.

Through valleys of pure delight,
Where shadows dare not creep,
In the echoes, we unite,
In memories we keep.

Euphoria paints the skies,
With colors of hope and grace.
In the realm where spirits rise,
We find our sacred place.

Celestial Colorplay

Stars emerge in twilight's glow,
Painting dreams on velvet night.
Cosmic hues in waltz and flow,
A symphony of pure delight.

Planets spin with gentle grace,
In a dance of endless time.
Galaxies, they interlace,
Creating rhythms, soft and prime.

Comets trail with fiery spark,
Leaving whispers in the dark.
Each flicker tells a story bold,
Of secrets known and tales untold.

In celestial colorplay,
We find the magic in the skies.
As night turns slowly into day,
We glimpse eternity's disguise.

Chasing Chroma

Through fields of vibrant bloom,
Color bursts with fervent glee.
Each petal, a note from the womb,
Of nature's pure symphony.

We run where the rainbows bend,
Chasing shades of light and dream.
In the spectrum, we transcend,
Flowing like a silent stream.

Every hue, a story spun,
In the tapestry of earth.
With each glance, a new begun,
Revealing beauty's worth.

Chasing chroma, hearts ignite,
In this dance of endless play.
Colors weave through day and night,
Guiding us along the way.

Tides of Tonality

Waves crash in a soothing song,
Melodies of the sea's embrace.
Harmony flows, swift and strong,
In the chorus of time and space.

Echoes drift on ocean breeze,
Notes that sparkle, fade and rise.
In the cadence, hearts find ease,
As the water whispers sighs.

Each tide, a verse to unfold,
In the rhythm of the deep.
Stories of the brave and bold,
In tranquility, we leap.

Tides of tonality blend,
Crafting dreams in fluid lines.
In this dance, let us transcend,
Holding peace as love entwines.

Celestial Canvas

Stars drip like paint from the night,
Galaxies swirling in endless flight.
Nebulas bloom in colors aglow,
On this canvas where dreams overflow.

Heavens whisper secrets untold,
In silken threads of silver and gold.
Each stroke of light a story shared,
In the vastness, all souls are bared.

Moons play hide and seek with the sun,
Chasing shadows till the night is done.
In twilight's embrace, the colors blend,
A masterpiece where the bright stars mend.

Wonders of space in splendor reside,
On this canvas where hearts confide.
With every glance, a wish does soar,
In the celestial dance, forevermore.

Hues of Hope

Soft pastels paint the morning sky,
As dreams awaken, spirits fly.
From dawn's blush to twilight's glow,
In each hue, hope starts to grow.

Emerald greens and sapphire blues,
A palette rich with vibrant views.
Through every stroke, the heart ignites,
In the canvas of our endless nights.

Sunset whispers promises near,
In shades of amber, bright and clear.
Each color tells of futures bright,
As we weave our dreams in light.

With every brush, a tale unfolds,
In brushstrokes bold and colors gold.
A dance of hues that inspires the soul,
In this vibrant world, we find our role.

Emotion's Kaleidoscope

Feelings spiral in colors so bright,
A dance of tones in the fading light.
Joy and sorrow blend, twist, and twine,
In a kaleidoscope of the heart's design.

Crimson laughter, azure tears,
Whirling together through the years.
Each fragment a story, a moment, a dream,
In shifting patterns, emotions teem.

Golden moments, shadows of gray,
Each hue revealing its own kind of sway.
Love's bright green, regretful brown,
In this tapestry, we wear our crown.

A whirl of feelings, both fierce and deep,
In the art of emotion, secrets we keep.
Through glass and light, we seek to find,
The beauty surrounding the heart and mind.

The Art of Emotion

In every heartbeat, a brushstroke flows,
On the canvas of life, an artist knows.
With shades of laughter, strokes of pain,
A masterpiece born from joy and rain.

Lines of passion, curves of grace,
Every emotion finds its place.
Created in moments, both dark and bright,
We paint our world with love's pure light.

The palette thick with memories dear,
Brushes dipped in the essence of fear.
Yet from the shadows springs forth the glow,
In the art of emotion, we learn and grow.

Every tear, a well of depth,
Every smile, a promise kept.
Through the strokes of our life's gentle hand,
We craft a story, a vibrant strand.

Melodies in Monochrome

In shades of gray, the whispers play,
Soft echoes linger, night turns to day.
A song of silence, sweet and rare,
Each note a brushstroke, hanging in air.

Life in contrast, bold yet meek,
A symphony of shadows that softly speak.
In every corner, memories twine,
Melodies drift, in rhythm divine.

With every heartbeat, colors blend,
A dance of twilight, where time won't end.
The serenade of dusk, a haunting call,
In monochrome dreams, we rise and fall.

Notes of Nostalgia

Distant echoes from days gone by,
Whispers of laughter, a gentle sigh.
Memories wrapped in a soft embrace,
Melodies linger, time can't erase.

Old records spin, the needle glides,
Each song a journey where heart resides.
Faded photographs, a tender thread,
Connecting moments, the words unsaid.

In every chord, a story wakes,
Of love and loss, of joys and aches.
Nostalgia dances, a bittersweet balm,
Cradled in tunes, the world feels calm.

Dancing with Dyes

Brush strokes of color, vivid and bright,
In a canvas of dreams, we take flight.
Swirls of passion, hues that ignite,
Dancing with dyes beneath the moonlight.

Every splash tells a tale anew,
In gardens of pigments, where thoughts accrue.
A waltz of wonder on fabric and skin,
Creating a masterpiece, where we begin.

With laughter and smiles, the colors bleed,
A tapestry woven with joyous seeds.
In the rhythm of art, our spirits soar,
Dancing with dyes forevermore.

Energized Embrace

In the morning light, we rise with grace,
A surge of energy in each embrace.
Hearts aligned, in rhythm we flow,
Dynamic forces, together we grow.

Laughter like thunder, a vibrant spark,
Illuminating paths that once were dark.
With every hug, the world expands,
A fusion of souls, with open hands.

In the warmth of love, we find our place,
Energized pulses, a fervent chase.
With every heartbeat, together we race,
In an endless dance, in an energized embrace.

Luminescence in the Quiet

In the stillness, whispers glow,
Soft secrets in the night they sow.
Stars awaken, one by one,
Guided by the silver sun.

Gentle breezes stir the trees,
Carrying tales on the breeze.
Moonlight dances on the floor,
Every shadow begs for more.

Silence speaks in colors bright,
Bringing warmth to the cold night.
Dreams unfurl with the dawn's embrace,
In the quiet, find your place.

In each heartbeat, a soft light,
Illuminates the edges tight.
Hold the moment, let it stay,
In luminescence, drift away.

Weaving Dreams with Light

Threads of gold in the sky spin,
Crafting visions where hopes begin.
Clouds like canvases float high,
Painting dreams for the wandering eye.

Twilight whispers, secrets abound,
In the fabric where dreams are found.
Every shimmer, a tale told,
In the tapestry, life unfolds.

Colors blend, create a spark,
Illuminating paths through the dark.
With each stroke, a story we weave,
In the embrace of night, believe.

Luminous threads in a soft hand,
Building castles in the sand.
Together we soar, hearts alight,
Weaving dreams with radiant light.

Illusions of Grief and Grace

In the silence, shadows creep,
Haunting moments that we keep.
Whispers of loss, softly trace,
The delicate line of grief and grace.

Tears like rivers, flowing wide,
Spaces where our pain can hide.
Yet in sorrow, beauty glows,
In the heart where compassion grows.

Time etches lines, a poignant art,
Every fracture, a work of heart.
In the echoes, we find embrace,
Illusions fade, revealing grace.

Through the darkness, a light appears,
Healing wounds beneath the tears.
In the dance of loss, we find peace,
And from the shadows, learn release.

Chromatic Echoes of the Past

Memory flickers like old film,
Colors vibrant yet dim.
Brushstrokes on a canvas worn,
In the shadows, stories born.

Echoes dance in twilight's glow,
Tracing paths we used to know.
Faded laughter in each hue,
Remnants of a life that flew.

In nostalgia, we find our place,
Fragmented moments we embrace.
Through the lens of time, we see,
Chromatic echoes setting free.

Past and present, intertwined,
In the heart, all is aligned.
From the spectrum, our souls rise,
In these echoes, we find skies.

Spectrum of Emotions

In the dawn, joy begins to rise,
A gentle warmth, a bright surprise.
Yet shadows lurk, with fears in tow,
A symphony of highs and lows.

Love can bloom in vibrant hues,
While sorrow paints in deepened blues.
Each feeling dances, bright and true,
A canvas rich in every hue.

Through laughter's echoes, tears can flow,
The heart, a river, fast or slow.
In moments fleeting, memories cling,
Life's a chorus, we all sing.

Embrace the chaos, let it rise,
For every storm, a brightened skies.
With each new wave, the colors blend,
In this great tapestry, we mend.

Shades of Solitude

In quiet corners, shadows loom,
Whispers echo in the room.
With pages turned, the clock ticks slow,
A world within begins to glow.

The moonlight bathes the empty streets,
Where solitude and stillness meet.
Each star a friend, a fleeting glance,
In silent nights, the heart will dance.

Through thoughts that wander, dreams take flight,
In shadows cast by soft starlight.
In solitude, we find our peace,
A sanctuary where fears cease.

Yet in this quiet, life persists,
A symphony of tender twists.
From shades of gray to colors bright,
In solitude, we find our light.

Tides of Colorful Whispers

Beneath the waves, secrets hide,
With whispers soft, like a gentle tide.
Coral dreams in ocean's sway,
Call to hearts, in sweet ballet.

In azure depths, stories untold,
Fish painted bright, in colors bold.
Dancing currents carry the tune,
A melody under the moon.

With each ebb and flow, a new embrace,
Nature's canvas, a vibrant space.
From foam and surf, to quiet sands,
Life is woven by unseen hands.

Embrace the whispers, heed the call,
In vibrant tides, we rise and fall.
Colorful tales in every wave,
In the ocean's heart, we find the brave.

Chasing Vivid Dreams

In the dawn's light, visions gleam,
A canvas stretched, we dare to dream.
With every heartbeat, hopes take flight,
Guided by stars in the velvet night.

Brush in hand, we paint the skies,
With strokes of courage, we sever ties.
Daring paths we choose to tread,
As vibrant futures dance ahead.

Through struggles faced, and mountains climbed,
In every setback, strength is rhymed.
A tapestry of goals and schemes,
We chase the threads of vivid dreams.

So run, dear heart, through fields of gold,
Let passion's fire be brightly bold.
For in the chase, we find our song,
In vivid dreams, we all belong.

Moods like Rainfall

Gentle drops on windowpanes,
Whispers of the soft refrain.
Cloudy hues and silver gleam,
Nature's dance in quiet dream.

Melancholy, sweet and bright,
Shadows flit in fading light.
Each patter sings a tender tune,
Heartbeats echo, afternoon.

Stormy gray or sunlit gold,
Emotions shifting, stories told.
In the silence, echoes play,
Moods like rainfall on display.

Cleansing soul with every sigh,
Through the ages, time goes by.
Let it fall, embrace the flow,
In the depths, let feelings grow.

Palette of Pulses

Colors bright and shadows deep,
In the heart, the visions leap.
Rhythms dance, a lively breeze,
Painting life with sweetest ease.

Brush of warmth and touch of cool,
Life's a canvas, love the tool.
Every heartbeat, every sigh,
Artistry that can't deny.

With a stroke, the world ignites,
Splashes bold on starry nights.
Feel the pulses in the air,
Every hue, a love laid bare.

In this blend, we find our way,
Dancing colors, night and day.
A palette rich, forever true,
Painting dreams in every hue.

Radiant Reveries

In the garden of my mind,
Where daydreams bloom, both warm and kind.
Sunlit paths and starlit skies,
Whispers soft, the heart complies.

Every thought, a gentle ray,
Guiding light to find the way.
In the quiet, visions play,
Radiant tales in soft array.

Through the pages, words take flight,
In the depths of endless night.
Hopeful hearts and dreams alive,
In these reveries, we thrive.

Let the moments weave their spell,
In our souls, where wonders dwell.
Hold them close, let shadows fade,
In radiant hues, our lives are made.

Tints of Tranquility

Whispers float on evening's breeze,
Calm descends, the heart's at ease.
Pastel skies and gentle sighs,
In the quiet, peace will rise.

In the stillness, time slows down,
As daylight fades, we wear a crown.
Moments linger, soft and sweet,
Finding solace, life's retreat.

Tints of blue and shades of green,
In this haven, calm is seen.
Breathe it in, the fragrant air,
Tranquility beyond compare.

Let the world drift far away,
In these hues, I yearn to stay.
Wrapped in comfort, heart in hand,
Tints of tranquility, so grand.

Symphony of Shades

In twilight's glow, colors blend,
Whispers of dusk, a soft commend.
Shadows dance, a gentle sway,
Harmonies of night and day.

Cascading light in tender streams,
Painting life in whispered dreams.
Each hue sings a tale untold,
In silence rich, in beauty bold.

The canvas grows, a living sound,
Echoes of life weave all around.
With every brush, a note is born,
A symphony of dusk and dawn.

As stars emerge, they paint the skies,
With silver strokes, the night complies.
In this embrace, we find our place,
Where colors meet, the heart's grace.

Brushstrokes of Bliss

In sunlit fields, joy takes flight,
Each stroke a dance, a pure delight.
Colors twirl, in vibrant air,
With every hue, we shed our care.

A palette bright with nature's art,
Brushstrokes fill the beating heart.
Each curve and line, a story spun,
In every shade, we see the sun.

As laughter blooms in shades of bright,
We chase the day, we hold the light.
In gentle whispers, joy conveys,
The beauty found in simple ways.

With every stroke, a world awakes,
In blissful moments, the heart breaks.
Embrace the light, let colors sing,
In brushstrokes, find the joy we bring.

Euphoria's Embrace

In laughter's echo, spirits soar,
Joy spills freely, forevermore.
Each fleeting moment, a sweet delight,
In euphoria's arms, we take flight.

Sunset drapes the sky in gold,
A warm embrace, where dreams unfold.
The heart ignites with every glance,
In twilight's realm, we find our chance.

A gentle breeze carries our song,
In nature's cradle, we belong.
With every beat, the world aligns,
In unity, the soul defines.

So let us dance, let spirits rise,
In euphoria's glow, love never lies.
With open hearts, we find our ways,
In radiant light, through endless days.

Colorful Journeys

Upon the path where colors play,
Each step reveals the bright array.
Through fields of green and skies of blue,
In every journey, life feels new.

With every turn, new shades ignite,
From dawn to dusk, the world feels bright.
In valleys deep, on mountains high,
Adventure calls, beneath the sky.

Through winding roads and rivers clear,
In every moment, joy draws near.
With every brush, life's colors blend,
In colorful journeys, hearts transcend.

So take a step, let colors bloom,
In every heart, let love consume.
In hues of life, we find our way,
In vibrant journeys, come what may.

Spectrum of Sentiments

In hues of joy and shades of grey,
Where laughter meets the tears we fray.
A rainbow painted on the soul,
Each color telling stories whole.

A silent sigh, a thunder's roar,
Echoes of what we can't ignore.
The heartbeats blend in soft embrace,
A spectrum found in every space.

Moments flicker like fireflies,
Underneath the endless skies.
In whispers held by nature's grace,
Each sentiment finds its own place.

From blissful highs to valleys deep,
The tapestry of life we keep.
Through every turn and winding street,
In love and loss, our hearts compete.

Vibrant Whispers

In gentle winds that softly play,
Vibrant whispers find their way.
Through trees that sway, in sunlight's gleam,
They carry forth our hidden dream.

A dance of leaves, a playful breeze,
Whispers of love that never cease.
In every murmur, secrets lie,
Soft echoes traced beneath the sky.

The laughter carried on the streams,
Unwritten tales of bygone dreams.
In every moment, life ignites,
Vibrant whispers, the heart's delights.

With each new dawn, their stories bloom,
Filling the world with sweet perfume.
In every corner, joy persists,
Vibrant whispers, the soul's lsts.

Canvas of Chaos

On a canvas filled with strokes of fate,
Chaos dances, never too late.
Colors clash and shapes collide,
Each mess reveals what we can't hide.

With darkened clouds and bursts of light,
A masterpiece born from endless fight.
Emotion flows in wild array,
A canvas telling what words can't say.

In splatters bright, in shadows dim,
Life creates its own daring hymn.
Each chaotic twist and turn we trace,
A vivid journey, a frantic race.

Yet in the madness, beauty lies,
A revelation bold that defies.
For every scar, a story's spark,
In chaos blooms the brightest art.

Dances of Delight

In twilight's glow, the stars appear,
Dancing softly, drawing near.
With every twirl, the dreams take flight,
In the hush of the coming night.

A rhythm found in heartbeats' call,
Each note a story, one and all.
With laughter fluttering through the air,
Delight unfolds beyond compare.

Step by step, the souls align,
Across the floor, a waltz divine.
In every spin, a spark ignites,
As joy erupts, embracing lights.

Together held in life's embrace,
In dances of delight, we trace.
The moments cherished, pure and bright,
In every step, our hearts unite.

Burst of Butterflies

In gardens bright, they flit and fly,
Wings of whispers, painting the sky.
A dance of colors, soft and bold,
Nature's secrets in stories told.

They land on blooms, a fleeting guest,
Each gentle flutter, a treasured quest.
In moments lost, they weave a thread,
A tapestry where dreams are spread.

With every breeze, their laughter sighs,
Life in motion, where freedom lies.
A burst of joy, they bring and share,
In this fleeting gift, the world laid bare.

Letting Colors Speak

On canvas bright, emotions flow,
Brushes dance, setting hearts aglow.
Each shade and hue tells tales untold,
In every stroke, a passion bold.

Azure depths, like ocean's embrace,
Sunset oranges, a warm embrace.
Violet shadows blend with the night,
Inviting dreams to take their flight.

Let colors speak, let silence fade,
In every corner, memories laid.
Artistry's language, pure and true,
In vibrant whispers, life renews.

Hue-Shifting Moments

In twilight's glow, the colors shift,
As shadows blend and spirits lift.
From golden dawn to dusky night,
Each moment glimmers, pure delight.

Where cherry blossoms greet the spring,
And autumn leaves in crispness cling.
Nature's palette, always in tune,
Painting memories 'neath the moon.

With every breath, a new design,
In shifting hues, the stars align.
A journey bright, a constant change,
In life's embrace, we rearrange.

Sunlit Sorrows

Beneath the sun, we wear our grief,
In golden rays, we seek relief.
Yet shadows linger, tales untold,
In warmth of light, our hearts unfold.

A sunset's glow can hide the pain,
While rainbows form from tears like rain.
In every smile, a crack may show,
A tapestry where sorrow flows.

Through sunlit paths, we find our way,
Embracing joy within dismay.
For in the light, we learn to cope,
In sunlit sorrows, lies our hope.

Boulevard of Blues

Walking down this lonely street,
Whispers of the past retreat.
Echoes of laughter, shadows fade,
Memories linger, but won't invade.

Footsteps heavy, hearts unsure,
Searching for a fleeting cure.
Streetlights flicker, dreams collide,
In the silence, pain resides.

Lost in thoughts of what could be,
Underneath the darkened tree.
Hope shines dim but still persists,
On this boulevard, love's sweet mist.

Yet through the blues, a spark will glow,
A flickering flame amid the woe.
For every tear that falls like rain,
A new beginning can still remain.

Carousels of Color

Round and round the colors spin,
A vibrant dance of joy within.
Painted horses, bright and bold,
Tales of wonder still untold.

Laughing children, faces bright,
Chasing dreams in pure delight.
Every turn, a new surprise,
In this realm where magic lies.

Swirls of red and shades of blue,
Every glance feels fresh and new.
Moments captured in a glance,
In this world, we lose ourselves in dance.

As the music softly plays,
Carousels drift on bright arrays.
Life's a ride, let colors sing,
In every heart, the joy they bring.

Infused Emotions

Deep within the quiet night,
Embers glow, a flickering light.
Thoughts entwine like vines that clutch,
Feelings bloom with tender touch.

Joy and sorrow dance as one,
Underneath the velvet sun.
Heartbeats echo, silence breaks,
In this realm, the soul awakes.

Each emotion paints the sky,
Scarlet dreams that soar up high.
Canvas filled with hopes and fears,
Brushstrokes whisper lost desires.

In this interplay of shades,
Vivid tales that time cascades.
Traverse the depths, embrace the flow,
In infused emotions, we truly grow.

Radiance of Longing

In the twilight's gentle glow,
Whispers of a love we know.
Stars appear, they softly gleam,
Echoes of a distant dream.

Lingering in the dusky air,
Yearning hearts find solace there.
Every glance, a sweet embrace,
Memories linger, leave a trace.

With each heartbeat, hope ignites,
Carving paths through endless nights.
Radiance shines from deep inside,
In longing's light, our souls abide.

As the dawn begins to break,
Promises of love we make.
Through the shadows, love will rise,
In radiance, our spirits fly.

Shimmering Shadows

In the twilight the shadows dance,
Whispers of night, a mystic trance.
Softly they glide on the silver streams,
Carrying secrets of moonlit dreams.

Underneath the starlit sky,
They flicker and fade, then gently sigh.
A world unseen, where spirits weave,
Shimmering hopes that we believe.

Through the mist, they play their part,
Echoes of light that touch the heart.
In every corner, the shadows blend,
A tapestry of night without end.

Embracing darkness, they bring us peace,
In their presence, all worries cease.
Shimmering shadows, a gentle guide,
In their depths, we can confide.

Sails of Sentiment

On waves of dreams, our thoughts set sail,
With every breeze, we tell a tale.
The sea of feeling, vast and true,
Our hearts the compass, forever due.

Through storms and calm, we navigate,
Emotions rise, we oscillate.
With each swell, a new refrain,
In sails of sentiment, we remain.

Anchored in love, we find our way,
Guided by stars that gently sway.
In the quiet depths, we hear a call,
Together we rise, never to fall.

In every harbor, our hearts align,
Upon the waters, our souls entwine.
With the winds of change, we'll glide and soar,
On sails of sentiment, forevermore.

Paintbrush of Passion

With every stroke, emotions flare,
Colors collide in the open air.
Dreams take shape upon the canvas,
Fleeting moments we hope to harness.

The hues of love, both bright and bold,
Stories waiting to be told.
In every line, a yearning plea,
A heart revealed, wild and free.

Splashes of joy, whispers of pain,
Each color drips like gentle rain.
Through the art, our spirits roam,
Finding in creation, a sense of home.

As we paint the world with our desires,
Igniting life with vibrant fires.
In this masterpiece, we find our way,
With the paintbrush of passion, come what may.

Rainbow Whispers

Beneath the arch of vibrant skies,
Colors blend where silence lies.
Whispers float on the gentle breeze,
Carried softly through rustling trees.

Each hue a story, a dream unfurled,
Painting the heart of a weary world.
In tender moments, they intertwine,
Rainbow whispers, both yours and mine.

When storms have passed and calm prevails,
We find ourselves on colorful trails.
With every step, we chase the light,
In the embrace of day and night.

Unseen connections, a luminous thread,
In every whisper, the love we've spread.
Let the colors guide us, forever true,
In rainbow whispers, me and you.

Hues of Heartbeats

In twilight's glow, soft whispers rise,
Each pulse a brush on canvas skies.
Colors dance where shadows lie,
Painting dreams that float and fly.

A crimson throb, a gentle sigh,
Moments captured, dancing high.
With every beat, a story told,
In vibrant strokes, the heart unfolds.

Emerald greens and sapphire blues,
Every heartbeat, a different muse.
Underneath the starlit dome,
Each hue a step, each step a home.

In stillness found, emotions spill,
A spectrum bright, a silent thrill.
As night dissolves into the dawn,
The hues of heartbeats linger on.

Tones of Turmoil

In restless winds, the shadows play,
Chaos reigns where silence sways.
Each note a cry, a haunting sound,
As tempests gather all around.

The thunder rolls, a song of fate,
In darkest nights, we contemplate.
With every clash, our hopes collide,
In storms of doubt, we try to hide.

A symphony of fear and fire,
Echoes build, drawing higher.
Lines of struggle, harsh and real,
Through discord's pain, we learn to heal.

Yet in the maelstrom, strength is found,
With every tremor, we rebound.
In the depths of turmoil's haze,
We seek the light, we find new ways.

Fleeting Fragments

Moments slip through fingers thin,
Like grains of sand, they swirl and spin.
Captured laughter, lost in time,
Whispers echo, reason and rhyme.

A flash of joy, a flicker of pain,
In fleeting fragments, we find our gain.
Memories dance, a soft lament,
What once was whole, now fragmented.

A glance, a smile, a distant stare,
In fleeting bits, we learn to care.
Each piece a story waiting to share,
In transient moments, the heart lays bare.

Chasing fragments, forever run,
In fleeting seconds, we become one.
Through time's embrace, we learn to see,
The beauty found in constancy.

Palette of Playfulness

With splashes bright and colors bold,
A playful heart, a story told.
In strokes of joy, the canvas sings,
A world of wonders, laughter brings.

Like sunshine beams on summer's day,
Imagination finds its way.
With every stroke, a smile appears,
Transforming worries into cheers.

A whimsical dance, a joyful spin,
In vibrant hues, the fun begins.
Creating tales where dreams ignite,
With playful spirits, we take flight.

In this palette where laughter thrives,
We paint the colors of our lives.
Each playful brush, a step we take,
A joyful journey, no heartache.

Cloud of Color

Fluffy whispers in the sky,
A vivid dance where dreams can fly.
Painted hues in sunlight's glow,
A canvas where soft breezes flow.

Glimmers of lavender and gold,
Stories of ages, silently told.
Brightness wraps the world in cheer,
A fleeting moment, precious and clear.

Crimson trails of sunset's light,
Embers fading into the night.
Colors merge, a soft embrace,
In the heavens, a glowing space.

As twilight descends with grace,
Stars appear in light's warm space.
A cloud of color, soft and free,
Whispering secrets to you and me.

Spectrum of Sighs

In muted tones, the heart expresses,
Whispers woven in soft caresses.
Each sigh a note in a gentle song,
Colors blend, though the path feels long.

Mellow shades of pale and deep,
Echoes of promises we keep.
With every breath, a tone to share,
A spectrum woven with utmost care.

Faded hues of laughter past,
Moments cherished, shadows cast.
A gentle ebb, a soothing flow,
In the spectrum, emotions glow.

Each sigh a brushstroke of our days,
In vibrant shades, love's tender gaze.
A tapestry of feelings so wide,
In the palette of life, we confide.

Touch of the Tonal

A golden ray touches the tree,
Light breaks gently, wild and free.
With every tone that fills the air,
Nature hums a melody rare.

In the rustle of leaves, a song,
Vibrant chords where dreams belong.
The wind whispers soft, inviting grace,
In the realm of sound, we find our place.

Each note dances on sunlit streams,
Crafting echoes of our dreams.
A symphony played by earth and sky,
In this touch, we learn to fly.

With colors bright and sounds aglow,
The heart beats where the rhythms flow.
In each moment, a spark ignites,
A tonal touch, the world delights.

Chromatic Journey

Step into hues of every shade,
A chromatic path that dreams have laid.
From dawn's first light to twilight's rest,
In colors, we are gently blessed.

Wander through fields of emerald green,
Feel the whisper of what has been.
Each step a shade, each breath a tone,
In this journey, we are never alone.

From sapphire skies to ruby nights,
Every moment holds endless sights.
With every heartbeat, colors blend,
In this dance, our souls transcend.

Embrace the journey, let it unfold,
Paint your story in shades of bold.
In the tapestry of life so bright,
We find our peace in color's light.

Fragments of Flair

In whispers soft, the colors blend,
Pieces of dreams, around the bend.
Bright starlight dances, shadows play,
Fragrant moments fade away.

With every hue, a story spun,
Mosaic hearts, together run.
Glimmers caught in twilight's grace,
Life's canvas etched in time and space.

Each fragment tells a vibrant tale,
Where laughter echoes, love won't fail.
In silken threads, our worlds entwine,
In these fragments, hearts align.

Flecks of gold in azure skies,
Painted hopes where passion lies.
With every brush, we craft our fate,
In fragments bright, we celebrate.

Aurora of Affection

The dawn arrives, with blush and hue,
Kissing the earth, a love so true.
Stars retreat, the sun ascends,
In morning light, the heart amends.

Each ray that breaks the nighttime's hold,
Wraps us warm, with tales untold.
In gentle whispers, the day begins,
A symphony where love never ends.

Golden hues, like sweet caress,
In every moment, we feel blessed.
The world awakens, alive and bright,
In this aurora, hearts take flight.

Together we rise, beneath the skies,
In tender dawn, our spirits fly.
Each heartbeat matched in soft embrace,
In the aurora's glow, we find our place.

Shades that Sing

In twilight's grasp, the colors hum,
A harmony of life begun.
Each shade a note, a melody,
In shadows deep, we dance so free.

From violet dreams to sapphire seas,
The spectrum flows like whispering trees.
With every brush, the world awakes,
As silent songs the stillness breaks.

Emerald leaves in golden light,
The canvas turns from day to night.
In every hue, a chorus flies,
As shades that sing paint evening skies.

A palette rich, emotions blend,
In every stroke, our hearts extend.
Together we weave this sacred ring,
In the art of life, the shades that sing.

Tender Tints

Soft pastels float on gentle air,
Whispers of love are everywhere.
In peach and lavender's embrace,
Tender tints dance with grace.

Each shade a kiss upon the cheek,
In muted tones, our spirits speak.
With strokes so light, we find our way,
In tender tints, we choose to stay.

Faded hues of longing sigh,
Beneath the canvas of the sky.
With every brush, a dream takes form,
In tender tints, our hearts feel warm.

From early dusk to starry night,
Embracing every shade of light.
In every whisper, love's intent,
In tender tints, our time is spent.

Lost in Luminance

In the glow of twilight's gleam,
Shadows dance on a silver stream.
Whispers of the day still linger,
Like a soft-touch, a gentle finger.

Stars awaken, one by one,
Hiding secrets, lost from the sun.
Hearts aglow with dreams untold,
Guides us through the night so bold.

Each flicker, a promise made,
Paths illuminated, never to fade.
In the silence, we find our way,
Lost in luminance, come what may.

Vibrant Vulnerability

Petals open in the morning light,
Softly trembling, delicate sight.
In the breeze, a gentle sway,
Vibrant hues, where fears betray.

Exposed to storms, we learn to stand,
With open hearts, we reach for land.
Every scar, a story spun,
In this web, we are all one.

Embrace the rawness, let it show,
Nurture seeds of strength to grow.
In vulnerability, we find our voice,
Boldly shining, we rejoice.

Mosaics of Memory

Fragments of time, a shattered glass,
Colorful stories, moments pass.
Each piece fits in a wondrous way,
Crafting a picture of yesterday.

Echoes of laughter, shadows of tears,
Whispers of hopes drowned in fears.
Each heartbeat marks a trail we roam,
In the heart's canvas, we find our home.

Nostalgic whispers color the night,
Guiding us back, igniting the light.
Mosaics shimmer, forever entwined,
In the gallery of the mind.

Twists of Temperature

The sun dips low, the world turns cool,
Sipping warmth from the evening's jewel.
A dance of heat, a shiver of frost,
In nature's embrace, we feel the cost.

Storms brew fierce, then gentle rains,
Nature's heartbeat in ebbing pains.
In every twist, we find our way,
Changing seasons, both night and day.

Tempers rise in the summer's glare,
Chilling winds leave the earth laid bare.
With every shift, life renews its form,
In the beauty of change, we transform.

Iridescent Dreams

In the quiet night, stars align,
Whispers of hope, dreams intertwine.
Colors that shimmer, softly they gleam,
Carried on sighs, an iridescent dream.

Moonlight dances on silver streams,
Each flicker evokes forgotten themes.
Hearts drifting softly through vivid skies,
Awakening wonders with luminous sighs.

A tapestry woven of wishes and light,
Guiding our souls into tranquil night.
Every hue tells a story so bright,
In iridescent dreams, we take flight.

Eternal echoes of the heart's embrace,
Moments suspended in time and space.
Together we wander, forever we roam,
In this realm of dreams, we find our home.

Cascade of Feelings

Rushing waters, emotions collide,
In a cascade where secrets abide.
Gentle ripples, joy, and sorrow,
Flowing together, shaping tomorrow.

Whispers of love in every stream,
Carving through valleys, fulfilling a dream.
Each drop a story, both bitter and sweet,
In this waterfall, hearts gently meet.

Crashing feelings, wild and free,
Echoes of laughter, shadows of glee.
Carried away on currents so strong,
In the cascade of feelings, we belong.

Through the turbulence, soft moments sneak,
Words unspoken, yet feelings speak.
Together we journey, through highs and lows,
In the heart's cascade, true love grows.

Vivid Valleys

In the embrace of vibrant lands,
Nature's palette, crafted by hands.
Colors blooming beneath the sun,
In vivid valleys, our hearts are one.

Waves of flowers in the breezy air,
Each petal whispers, gentle and rare.
Mountains stand proud, a sheltering grace,
In every corner, the world's warm embrace.

Trickling streams weave stories untold,
Magic unfolds in shades bold.
Through rocky paths, our spirits soar,
In these vivid valleys, we long for more.

Every sunset ignites the skies,
Painting horizons where love never dies.
In the heart of nature, lose track of time,
In vivid valleys, life's joys chime.

Chromatic Confessions

With every brush, the truth reveals,
Artistry flows, a canvas feels.
Colors unravel the silent fears,
In chromatic confessions, truth appears.

Strokes of passion, splashes of pain,
Each hue a story, love's sweet gain.
Emotions dance in colorful beams,
In the palette of life, we paint our dreams.

Shades of longing, whispers of grace,
In vibrant tints, we find our place.
Every color speaks, a voice profound,
In chromatic confessions, hope is found.

As shadows blend with light's embrace,
In this spectrum, hearts find their space.
Together we share our deepest strife,
In the colors of truth, we find our life.

Unveiling the Hidden Spectrum

In shadows deep, the colors hide,
Unseen whispers, a vibrant tide.
Through the veil, we seek the light,
A dance of hues, both bold and bright.

From the black to the purest white,
Every shade tells a secret right.
A spectrum wide, a tale unfurled,
Revealing truths, unseen by the world.

Electric blues and fiery red,
The stories woven, softly said,
In every tint, a feeling blooms,
Painting dreams in silent rooms.

So lift the veil, and let it show,
The hidden spectrum we all know.
In every heart, a painter's hand,
Creating worlds, where colors stand.

Colors of Emotion

Crimson joy in laughter's flight,
Gentle blues in calm of night.
Greens of hope, the woods bestow,
Every hue with tales to show.

Gold of warmth in sunny days,
Silver tears that softly blaze.
Faded grays when sorrows creep,
Each color promises to keep.

Violets deep, with dreams entwined,
Yellows bright, where love is blind.
Through the palette, life unwinds,
In every stroke, a heart it finds.

So let us paint with pure devotion,
Explore the vastness of emotion.
In vibrant strokes, our souls confess,
The colors sing our happiness.

Hues of Heartstrings

Soft pastels, a whisper's call,
Saturated shades that rise and fall.
Each hue a note, a song's refrain,
Played gently on the heart's own grain.

Deep maroons where passions lie,
Tangerine dreams that soar and fly.
Muted tones of longing's sigh,
Brush strokes that time cannot deny.

Cobalt spark in moments fun,
Lavender twilight, day is done.
In every color, a thread connects,
Stitching stories, love reflects.

Let the palette of life unfold,
With every shade, a tale retold.
In the gallery of heart's delight,
Hues of heartstrings shine so bright.

Shades of Serenity

Soft aquas whisper to the soul,
Gentle grays and whites make whole.
Where the stillness meets the shore,
Each calm hue, a tranquil score.

Pale yellows of the morning light,
Bronze sunsets fade into the night.
Lavender fields under the stars,
Serenity found in hidden bars.

Silvery mists wrap the dawn,
Breezy greens on the soft lawn.
In the silence, colors breathe,
In every shade, sweet peace beneath.

So let us linger where light flows,
Among the shades, where silence grows.
In every breath, a gentle plea,
To find the quiet, to simply be.

Palette of Heartbeats

In shades of crimson, love does bloom,
Whispers echo in the quiet room.
Brush strokes linger, soft and bright,
Dancing shadows in the fading light.

Each heartbeat paints a story clear,
Colors mixed with every tear.
A canvas rich with dreams so bold,
A palette of the heart unfolds.

Through tangled threads of joy and pain,
Artistry is found in every stain.
With every passion, shades will blend,
Creating worlds that never end.

So let us mix our hues tonight,
And let our hearts take vibrant flight.
For in this art, we find our way,
A palette bright, come what may.

Echoes of a Prismatic Dawn

As the sun rises, colors burst,
In whispers sweet, the dreams immersed.
Each ray a promise stretched so wide,
Dew-kissed petals greet the tide.

Echoes dance in morning's glow,
Chasing shadows, time moves slow.
Pastel skies and clouds in flight,
Awake the world to soft daylight.

With every hue, a story told,
In silence, warmth begins to unfold.
Nature sings a vibrant tune,
As daybreak calls beneath the moon.

So let us wander far and free,
In echoes of what's meant to be.
For in this dawn of colors bright,
We find our dreams take wondrous flight.

Hues of Unspoken Desires

Hidden colors lie within,
A canvas blank where thoughts begin.
With gentle strokes, we dare to share,
The hues of hearts that linger there.

In whispers soft, our secrets blend,
A tapestry that knows no end.
Each brush creates a silent plea,
A spectrum yearning to be free.

Underneath the layers thick,
Lies the truth, and time does tick.
Unspoken dreams in every shade,
In vibrant light, our fears will fade.

So let us paint with tender care,
The unspoken desires that we bear.
For in each stroke, we'll find the way,
To bring our hearts to light of day.

Dance of the Chromatic Soul

In swirling shades, the heart takes flight,
With every twist, it sparks the night.
Colors thrive in a gentle sway,
As souls unite in rhythmic play.

Whirling patterns, vibrant and bold,
Tales of life in hues unfold.
The dance of dreams beneath the stars,
Reminds us who we truly are.

Each step a brush upon the floor,
A symphony we can't ignore.
Together we create our fate,
In colors deep, we celebrate.

So join the dance where colors blend,
In every heartbeat, let love mend.
With chromatic souls that intertwine,
A dance of life, forever divine.

The Arc of Intangible Spirits

In twilight's grasp, they dance and sway,
Whispers of echoes in soft ballet.
Shadows entwined in a gentle breeze,
Carrying secrets of ancient trees.

Chasing the mist in a silver stream,
Fleeting visions of a long-lost dream.
They sparkle faintly like stars that gleam,
A tapestry woven from thought and theme.

Through the silence, they wander and roam,
Guiding lost souls towards their true home.
With each silent step, they softly weave,
An arc of stories we barely perceive.

Their laughter lingers like dew on grass,
In the heart's silence, they gently pass.
A fleeting glimpse, like a breath of air,
Intangible spirits beyond compare.

Colors of Forgotten Laughter

Once vibrant hues now dulled with time,
Fleeting moments in dreams that climb.
Echoes of giggles lost in the breeze,
Carried away like rustling leaves.

Crayons of childhood strewn on the floor,
Sketches of joy we recall and adore.
Bright oranges and pinks start to fade,
Yet memories linger, sweet serenade.

Whispers of youth in a sunlit glow,
A palette of magic we used to know.
Under the stars, we painted our dreams,
In the canvas of night, laughter redeems.

As colors blend into shades that confer,
A symphony played by hearts that stir.
In the galleries of time, we find our way,
To dance in the colors of yesterday.

Rainfall of Deep Reflections

Drops fall softly like thoughts in the night,
Each a mirror, shimmering bright.
Puddles gather the weight of the sky,
Carrying whispers, a gentle sigh.

Waves of water in a delicate form,
Reflecting the world in its quiet storm.
Leaves dance lightly as rivers embrace,
In this stillness, we find our place.

Clouds float by with secrets untold,
Painting the earth in silver and gold.
In every drop, a universe flows,
Stories and dreams in gentle repose.

The rainfall brings solace, a sweet release,
Time to ponder, a moment of peace.
In the depths of the silence, we stand still,
Finding ourselves in the heart's quiet thrill.

The Symphony of Kaleidoscope Hearts

In patterns shifting, colors unite,
A symphony born in the depths of night.
Each heartbeat echoes a timeless refrain,
Melodies sung in joy and in pain.

Fragments of laughter, shards of despair,
Blend together with harmonies rare.
In the cacophony, a rhythm finds place,
A kaleidoscope dance, an embrace of grace.

Whirling together through shadows and light,
The symphony whispers of day and of night.
In every pulse, there's a story to tell,
Of hearts intertwining, where feelings dwell.

Let the music flow and carry us high,
In the symphony's arms, we learn to fly.
Kaleidoscope hearts in a dazzling show,
Find their freedom, in love's warm glow.

Milton Keynes UK
Ingram Content Group UK Ltd.
UKHW022006131124
451149UK00013B/1030